UNTITLED PAIN

MONIQUE JONES

ISBN: 978-1-6847-1373-8 (sc)
ISBN: 978-1-6847-1372-1 (e)

Lulu Publishing Services rev. date: 01/09/2020

FOR MY CHILDREN

FAROUQ

FAQUAN

JANUARY

Contents

Dedication ix

Vera 1

Monuette 21

Cathy 33

About the Author 59

Dedication

I dedicate this book to all women that empower and encourage other women. I dedicate this to the women that are not blinded and influenced by what they see but are strengthen by what they can't see. I'm talking about their faith in GOD. This book is for those who choose not to throw drinks and fight their sisters but to those who love, respect and give honors to their sisters. This book is for the women who do not slander their sisters but instead will pick their sisters up off the floor when she has fallen. This book is for the women that accompany their sisters to doctor's appointments, nursing homes, churches and cemeteries. We as women go through so many trials and struggles and we endure to the end because of the love and support of our sisters. Remember that GOD created women for greatness and when we stick together we can accomplish so much. Let us not let the enemy, Satan influence us to tear each other down. Instead let's continue to pray, encourage and support one another. The trick of the enemy is to keep us at odds with one another because he knows that we can accomplish so much together. That is why he came after Eve and not after Adam. Don't let the pride of life or the lust of the eyes have you to step on your sister or hold one another down like crabs in a barrel. GOD IS LOVE AND I LOVE YALL!!!

Vera

It was a snowy day in the winter of 2014 and Atlanta was shut down. Vera was scheduled to go into the hospital for her chemotherapy treatment this morning but the weather advisory was for everyone to stay indoors even the federal and state offices were closed today. In New York this amount of snow would have been called a dusting. As she lay in bed in a cold house she longed for the New York projects and the busy streets. So much had happened in the past few years.

Vera left New York two years ago following behind her boyfriend Tony. Tony moved to Atlanta to become a rap artist and a reality television star but was now serving time in prison. Vera had to sell everything including her body to pay for Tony's trial lawyer. He lost the trial and was now serving fifteen years in prison. Vera knew that Tony was a con artist, a scammer and drug dealer when she had first met him in New York years before. They met at Sin City a club where Vera once danced.

One evening Tony invited Vera into his V.I.P. section where he and his friends spent on average $9,000 for bottles of Champagne, liquor and dancers every time they came to the club. One night Vera left with Tony and they were together ever since that night.

After several months of them as an item he told her to quit dancing and he moved her into his condo in Harlem. Vera moved out of the apartment in the projects in which she lived with her Mom and her siblings. Vera got "brand new" after she started going steady with Tony. She changed on her family, friends and the ladies that she once danced with. Tony bought her a Range Rover, diamonds, furs, designer shoes and bags and because he was a scammer he paid for it all with fraudulent credit cards and drug money. He would also give her fake credit cards which they called "swipes" on a daily basis for her to shop and eat with. They began going to Sin City together. Now Vera was treating the dancers that she once danced with as if they were beneath her. Vera forgot that she only had a tenth grade education and no job skills. The only other job she ever had besides dancing was babysitting.

Tony invested some money in a recording studio and started rapping. When he released his first mixtape he began getting airtime on all the major radio stations in Philadelphia, New York, North Carolina, Georgia, Miami and Chicago. He received offers to perform his hit song “SHE’S NOT A BUM, BUT SHE’S DUMB” in clubs from Philadelphia to Miami. He was on top and about to sign a record deal with a major record label in Atlanta.

Tony was still connected to the streets though. Rapping didn’t give him the same rush that he got from hustling and scamming. So when he was offered to sign the record deal in Atlanta he had already decided to bring his crew along so they could do what they had been doing in New York for years. Money was coming fast and he purchased a house in the Buckhead area of Atlanta with cash and furnished it with fake credit cards and fraudulent checks. Tony and his crew tore the town up dropping fraudulent checks and using fake credit cards everywhere they went. Tony received a $150,000.00 advance for signing with the record label in Atlanta but still longed for the drug money. Vera had become so materialistic and not once did she try to encourage Tony to turn his life around. Not once did she tell Tony to leave the street life alone and focus solely on his career as an artist. Vera enjoyed hanging with the reality television stars and attending award ceremonies. She thought it would last forever.

But one morning it all came to an end. The DEA and FBI were at the door with warrants for Tony and his entourage. They were all hauled off to jail. Vera was by Tony's side from his first arraignment until the end of the trial. In the end, Tony was convicted of drug trafficking, identity death and bank fraud. The record company released Tony of his contract because they said Tony was a "bad look" for the company. Before the trail he was refused bail because he was labeled a flight risk. Vera began to sell her jewelry, started dancing again and was dating customers in order to pay the household bills and Tony's trial lawyer.

Vera had noticed discharge from her breast and thought that she felt a lump in her left breast. "I'm pregnant" she thought to herself. She was getting tired, weak, and irritable so she decided to go see a doctor thinking that maybe she was pregnant. She knew she was under a lot of stress and was suffering from depression as well. When she saw the gynecologist he ordered blood tests and a mammogram. He also gave her a referral to see an oncologist. Vera had broke down crying and told the doctor all she had endured for the past two years. So he suggested that she see a psychologist as well. Two weeks after her initial visit with the oncologist Vera went in for a follow-up. The oncologist informed Vera that she had breast cancer. Vera could not believe what she was hearing. She saw the doctor's mouth moving but heard no words. Breast cancer? Is he saying something about a mastectomy? Did he say stage 3? Vera jumped up from the stretcher. What he was saying couldn't be true. She screamed, reached for her clothes and began to cry.

"I'm going to get a second opinion. I came here because I was tired, weak and depressed now you're telling me that I have stage 3 breast cancer? You're telling me to have my breast removed and I'm only Thirty-two years old." Vera was yelling and crying. The doctor and the nurse who had come into the room when she heard Vera's screams tried to calm Vera but she was now crying uncontrollably.

"Miss White, it is your prerogative to have a second

opinion. If you need a referral I will give you one to be seen at another hospital in Atlanta. I'm also going to give you the number to my office. My secretary's name is Brittany, leave a message for me if you want and I will return your call at my earliest convenience." said the doctor.

Vera made an appointment to see an oncologist at Piedmont hospital. Her appointment was scheduled two weeks away and during that two weeks she almost lost her mind. She couldn't sleep and was drinking alcohol and smoking weed constantly in an attempt to ease the pain. After seeing the oncologist at Piedmont hospital and having preliminary tests done it was confirmed that Vera did indeed have stage 3 breast cancer. She also needed to have an MRI done right away to see if the cancer had spread to the lymph nodes. Vera liked Piedmont Hospital better than Grady so she decided not to return to Grady Hospital.

The cancer hadn't spread to her lymph nodes so the Oncologist's plan of treatment was the double mastectomy followed by chemotherapy and reconstructive surgery afterwards. Vera didn't have any health insurance so she was assigned a social worker to help her with that. The social worker also told Vera about a support group that met at the hospital and in each others homes from time to time. Vera decided to give her mother and her sister a call to let them know what was going on and to see if one of them would come to stay with her while she went through this process. She had tried reaching out to them when Tony had first got arrested and offered to pay for someone's airfare if they would come stay with her. Unfortunately, for her they were still upset with her because she had turned her back on them when her and Tony were living the life of the rich and famous. Secretly, they prayed on Vera's downfall and said she was dead to them when old friends and family asked about Vera. Still she felt that this was different and that they would surely want to be with her now. She dialed the number and when her sister answered the phone Vera burst out crying and tried to explain what was going on in between the sobs. Her sister informed her that her mother was not available and went on to tell Vera that neither of them would come to Atlanta. She went on to tell her to ask her reality television friends.

The friends that Vera had ran with when her and Tony first came to Atlanta no longer invited her to dinner, parties or other social events. When her new friends realized she could no longer afford to pay for V.I.P. status the invites and calls stopped. Vera had no one to go through this process with. She looked forward to Tony's phone calls he helped lift her spirits even in the midst of his own situation. He encouraged her to attend the support group and to possibly make friends with a few of the women in the group.

So now as Vera lay in her bed in a cold house on a cold winter day she began to cry. She had never been this lonely in her life. She looked over at the pills on her bedside table and wanted to just take a handful and end it all. Even spending time at the infusion center was better than being home alone with no one to talk to. She didn't have cable television because she couldn't afford it so there was really nothing for her to watch on television. Suddenly her phone began to ring and she was hoping that her Mom or her sister was on the line but she didn't recognize the number.

"Hello" answered Vera.

"Hello, my name is Bridget I'm calling to speak to Vera. Is Vera available?"

"This is Vera"

"Hi Vera, again my name is Bridget. I'm one of the

ladies that attend the breast cancer support group at Piedmont Hospital here in Atlanta. I was just calling to see how you were making out today."

"I'm fine" lied Vera.

Bridget sensed something was wrong so she asked again.

"Are you sure you're doing okay? I get the feeling that you might not be okay." said Bridget.

At that moment the floodgates were open and Vera let out how she was really feeling.

"I'm just tired. I'm tired of everything. I just want to die! I'm tired of the nausea, I'm tired of the diarrhea, I'm tired of being alone in this house, I'm tired of Atlanta, I'm just tired" cried Vera.

"Last week I had my first round of chemo and I have to do this once a week for 4-6 months depending on the outcome. I can't work so I've been selling my jewelry, furniture and clothing to survive. I'm tired of struggling!"

Bridget just listened as Vera cried on the other end. "I miss my family. I know I was wrong for the way I treated my Mom and my sisters. They won't even give me a chance to apologize." Vera cried so hard that

Bridget could barely make out what she was saying but she listened more intently.

"It bothers me that my boyfriend Tony still has his family and friends and I'm alone in this house, in this town all alone. But now that I've started my Chemo I don't want to leave Atlanta until it's over."

Bridget spoke then "You may feel like you are alone but I want and need for you to know that GOD is always with you and now you have me. Our Cancer Support and Survivors group is awesome and I believe you will like all the women that attend. We are family and we do more than just meet once a week at the hospital. We shop, eat, trade recipes, go to the movies, barbeques and most of all we pray with and for each other."

"That sounds nice." Vera said through her sobs.

Bridget went on "The group has made me the official one woman welcoming committee. So after I saw your referral papers I decided to give you a call to introduce myself before this week's meeting and give you my contact information. Do you have a pen handy? You know what, you just relax and get yourself together. I'll call you tomorrow, okay?"

“Thanks for calling Bridget and I look forward to speaking with you tomorrow.”

“Vera, is it alright if I pray for you before we hang up?”

Okay, so she’s one of those religious types Vera thought to herself and twisted her face. Just when I thought I might have met a friend, now this. Vera rolled her eyes. Good thing Bridget couldn’t see her. She wanted to hang up the phone and act as if she lost her connection but something deep inside of her said. “That would be nice.”

Bridget began her prayer “Father God, I thank you for my new friend, your daughter Vera. Father I want to tell you how grateful I am for this day. The city of Atlanta is closed down but God you are still in charge and have allowed us to see this day. Father God we thank you for your healing power, we thank you for your grace and your mercy. God if you would allow me to bring forth and lift up the name of your daughter Vera. Father God, you know her pain so we ask for reconciliation in her family. I thank you God for the favor you have shown her thus far. God I thank you in advance for the financial breakthrough that she is about to receive. Father God, I thank you for protecting her and for protecting Tony while he is incarcerated. Father

God, I ask that you would lighten her burden and ease her pain. I ask this in the mighty name of Jesus. May the words of my mouth and the meditation of my heart be acceptable in your sight because Lord you are my strength and my redeemer. Amen."

In the weeks that followed Vera continued her chemotherapy. It made her nauseous, gave her diarrhea and one morning she awoke to find that her hair had fallen out. There was hair all over the pillow. Vera lost her mind and screamed. She ran into the bathroom to look in the mirror and when she saw her reflection she fell to her knees and began to cry. She reached for her cell phone and called Ms. Bridget. As soon as Bridget answered the phone Vera cried into the phone.

"My hair is falling out!!! I have bald spots all over my head. I can't take it anymore! I just want to die. I'm thirty-two years old with no titties and no hair. I just want to die!!!"

"Vera, don't say that! You have sat in enough groups to know that this was going to happen."

"Yes I have but I still wasn't prepared for this" Vera cried.

"I'll come over to your house. We'll go shopping for wigs and have lunch. See you shortly."

Bridget often invited Vera to Church and each time she invited her Vera smiled and said no thanks. Vera hadn't been to Church since elementary school when she often attended with her now deceased grandmother. Bridget was persistent in her asking though. She had made up her mind that this Sunday she was just going to drive out to Vera's house to get her. So on Sunday Bridget drove out to Vera's house and rang the doorbell. Vera had spotted Ms. Bridget's car as it approached the house so when Bridget rang the doorbell Vera opened the door right away and invited Ms. Bridget in. It wasn't the first time that Bridget had been to Vera's home, however, Bridget was in awe because the furnishings and artworks were now completely gone from the main floor.

"Good morning Ms. Bridget. What are you doing here?"

"I have come to take you to Church this morning. I'm not taking no for an answer either. So you just go ahead upstairs and get yourself together. I'll sit down here in the kitchen to wait for you."

"Uh, Ms. Bridget, I no longer have a kitchen set for you to sit down. I sold it but you can come upstairs there is a window seat where you can sit while I get dressed."

"Okay, come on girl let's get a move on" Bridget laughed.

Vera was trying to find something suitable for church. All of her shirts and blouses were low cut. She used to like to show off her D cup tits. In the end she settled for one of Tony's button up shirts, a pair of jeans and her Christian Louboutin heels. Just yesterday she had decided that she would soon put these shoes along with several others on ebay. She put on one of the wigs that Tina, a member of the support group had given her. Vera looked at herself in the bathroom mirror and decided that if she didn't go to Church today she may never go. She didn't like what she saw in the mirror but she had to admit that she looked better than she did three weeks ago at least she was able to smile now. She walked out of her bedroom and Bridget smiled.

"What is that I see in your eyes? There is life in you Vera!" Bridget said full of enthusiasm.

"Ms. Bridget you play too much" Vera said with a smile.

"C'mon let's go. We'll grab something to eat on the way."

Bridget knew that Vera did not have much money for food. She was practically living off of Ramen noodles. Once a month a nutritionist visited the support group and brought fresh fruits and vegetables from the local farmers market. The other ladies would give Vera some of their portion because they knew she was strapped for cash. This is how Vera got most of her vegetables.

The HOUSE OF PRAYER was located an hour away from Vera's house. They rode in Bridget's car and as they rode Bridget asked about Tony.

"He's doing better than me Ms. Bridget. He has no bills to pay, three meals a day and a bed to sleep on. His family and friends send him money from time to time and I write him on a regular basis."

"Vera, what is that I detect in your tone? Is it Jealousy, bitterness, or anger? Asked Bridget"

Vera sucked her teeth "Maybe all Ms. Bridget, maybe all."

Just then they were pulling into the Church parking lot so Bridget decided to drop the conversation for now.

As they entered the Church someone in the choir

was singing Yolanda Adams' OPEN MY HEART. Bridget took Vera over to her usual seat then focused her attention on the singer. Vera looked around, she was expecting a big church but the House Of Prayer was a small church with an intimate setting. Vera estimated it was about sixty people in attendance and that the church could seat one hundred and fifty people in the congregation and seven people on the platform.

After the woman finished singing, Pastor Monique Rutledge stepped to the podium. Bridget had spoken very highly of Pastor Rutledge and Vera wanted to see if all that Bridget had said was real.

"Thank you Sister Hall for that song this morning. I want us all to open up our hearts and minds and receive the word that God has for us today. Turn with me if you will to Luke chapter 15 verses 11-32 the story of the Prodigal Son."

The congregation opened their Bibles and turned to the scripture. Vera didn't have a bible so Bridget passed her's to Vera.

"If you have it say Amen" said Pastor Rutledge.

"Amen" said the congregation.

They all began to read and when they were finished Pastor Rutledge spoke again.

"This is the story of the prodigal son, however this could just as easily be your story. The prodigal mother, the prodigal father, the prodigal sister, the prodigal grandchild, the prodigal pastor."

The congregation chuckled when she said prodigal pastor. Pastor continued "You could laugh but the sad truth is that it has happened, pastors have left the church for many different reasons. But today I'm just going to call this sermon 'The Prodigals'. I believe that we all have heard about someone's family member running off to a far away land just to find themselves alone and in need of a one-way ticket home. The prodigals flee their homes for different reasons. Some for love, some for jobs, some for drugs and some are just fooled into believing they will have a better way of life. But these prodigals soon come to themselves and realize that they left home with the wrong intentions. In the scripture we find that the prodigal son was sleeping and eating with the pigs when he came to himself. In the Jewish tradition that was the lowest of the lowest to be with the swine. So I'm telling you that is how low these prodigals go before they return to our Father God. When their lover has left or they're fired from their job or maybe they just hit rock bottom and with no money and no food they finally humble themselves and seek the father, Father God. These prodigals realize that they just can't make it without Father God in their lives. So they call out 'Father help me!' They humble themselves and admit that they were wrong and cry aloud 'Father save me'"

Vera was in her seat crying. She knew she needed saving but she didn't know how to begin to even ask for help she didn't know how to pray either. Bridget passed her some tissues and put her arm around her shoulder. Vera was crying out loud now and the entire congregation looked her way.

"Please help me God!" cried Vera aloud.

Pastor Rutledge stopped speaking and motioned for Bridget to bring Vera forward. Some of the women in the church also walked towards the altar so that they could encircle Vera while Pastor Rutledge prayed for her.

Pastor prayed for Vera and when she was finished she led Vera in the sinner's prayer.

"Have you ever been baptized?" asked Pastor Rutledge.

"No" responded Vera.

"Well would you like to get baptized now that you have accepted Jesus as your Lord and Saviour?"

"Yes"

"Deaconess Mitchell will take you aside to get your information and to discuss baptism and your becoming a member of the House Of Prayer. This day is the beginning of a new life for you. Old things have passed away and now all things are new to you. God has forgiven you of your sins and your name has been added into the book of life. There is no need for you to go back and revisit the past sins because you are now a new person in Christ.

When church was over and Bridget and Vera were on their way home Vera said "Bridget you asked me a question before we got to church. I said maybe all but the truth was that I was bitter, angry and jealous about Tony's relationship with his family and friends but now it is all gone away. Bridget, I feel like a new person. You know I wanted to die, I wanted to just give up and call it quits but now I feel like I have hope. I feel like life is worth living. I'm going to give God a chance. I can't explain the feeling but if it was one word to describe how I was feeling I would say PEACE.

MONUETTE

Would this be the day she got dressed? Would she bathe today? Will she get out of bed to answer her door? Will she answer her phone? All these questions Monuette asked herself. It has been 5 days, 18 hours and 12 minutes since she buried her Mom. Two weeks prior to that Monuette and her Mom had buried Monuette's only brother Wayne and a month before that Monuette's mom, Lydia had to bury her only sister Dorothy.

Monuette was grief stricken. She could not stop crying. At times she felt as if she could not breath and the pain in her heart was unbearable. Her heart was truly aching an indescribable pain was in her heart that she would never be able to explain to anyone. At times she would just scream at the top of her lungs it was all she could do in between her sobs and her moans. She couldn't remember the last time that she had ate a meal. Then she remembered that the last time she ate was at her mom's repass and she only ate then because her friend Sabrina had practically forced it down her throat. Monuette was drinking a lot of water only because her throat was hoarse and dry from screaming out in agony.

Where was God? What kind of God would take her family away from her. Surely the loving God that she was raised to fear, love, praise and honor was not the God she thought he was. Monuette was angry with God right now and as she thought about her situation she began to cry out in agony. Once again she screamed and cursed God. Just then her phone rang but she ignored the call just as she had done for the past five days. She gathered that her message box was full by now and that there was no room for anyone to leave another message. She didn't care because she had no interest in speaking to anyone anyway.

She had taken time off of work when her brother Wayne was killed weeks ago. She had needed to be there for her Mom who was not over the sudden death of her only sister due to a ruptured aneurysm but now had to bury her only son. The news of Wayne getting hit by a stray bullet was shocking. Not just for the family but for the entire neighborhood and his friends in school. Wayne attended Penn State University and was currently taking his classes at the Hazelton campus. Wayne was due to receive his Bachelor's degree in May he majored in communications and had been offered an internship at CNN's New York location. On the night of January 8, 2016 Wayne while home in Harlem on break from school was on his way to meet with some of his friends from school for dinner in New York's meatpacking district and as he exited their apartment building on 140th street and Lenox Avenue he was caught in between a shoot out by two rivaling drug dealers. The bullet hit Wayne in the heart and he was killed instantly.

Lydia and Monuette couldn't believe what they were hearing when Wayne's childhood friend Benny came to tell them that Wayne was laid out on the sidewalk. The scream that Lydia let out when she saw Wayne's body will forever be etched in Monuette's memory. In the days that followed Lydia moved like a robot. Even now as Monuette recalled the events of the past weeks she did not know how Lydia had made it through. Monuette overheard Lydia crying and praying in the days that followed Wayne's death. Lydia had not given up her faith in God in the midst of her pain she remained grateful, thankful, joyful, prayerful and full of praise. Not Monuette, she was very angry that her only brother who was always giving, loving, and always ready to help was taken away from her. Why would God let him die? When her Mom would tell her to ask God to remove the pain Monuette would suck her teeth and walk away. She was full of anger and didn't want to hear that from her mother.

Now her Mom was gone. Lydia had been a member of Jesus The Christ Church for as long as Monuette could remember. She and Wayne would often say that Lydia spent more time at the church than at home. Lydia attended every Bible study, prayer meeting, deliverance service and worship service that she was able to. Mondays were the only evenings that Lydia was at home because there were no services on Mondays. She worked the front desk at the Crowne Plaza Hotel in Manhattan and after work she went straight to Jesus the Christ Church or JCC as the members called it. As children Monuette and Wayne attended JCC's after-school program so when Lydia reached the church after work they were already there on many occasions they would be in church until 11pm so the female members of JCC took turns bringing and preparing food for meals and snacks.

As Monuette lay in the bed sobbing she remembered her Mom saying "Never let rage find a resting place in your heart". How? How could she not be enraged at losing her entire family in two months? Her father had walked out on the family when Wayne was an infant. Wayne Scott Sr. had moved to Chicago and was never heard from again. Not be angry? How? How could she not want to scream at God. The tears began to burn in her eyes again as she thought of her upbringing, the doctrine she was taught and she remembered how faithful God was and how merciful he had been to her when she abandoned her beliefs and danced with the devil. Yes, Monuette had a past. Sex, drugs, gambling, alcohol, stripping, she had done it all. God was with her then was it possible that the same God who protected her then was with her now.

She rolled over in her bed and lit a cigarette. She had quit three years ago but picked up the habit again when Wayne was killed. Her mom prayed that it was a temporary outlet. As she inhaled the cigarette she thought of calling one of her friends that she used to party with. She still had their numbers and checked on them periodically and prayed for them often. She wanted to be numb, to feel nothing, to think of nothing. Some Hennessy, molly and weed would take care of that. She pulled on her cigarette and considered her options. "If you don't pick it up you won't get high!" she heard herself say. Was that her voice? She hadn't uttered words in five days. Oh she screamed and yelled and sobbed but she hadn't uttered words. "Get up!" she heard. There it was again her voice. Raspy, hoarse, scratchy but it was her voice. She snuffed out the cigarette in the ashtray on the nightstand. The ashtray overflowed with cigarette butts and the room reeked of cigarettes. After the repast Monuette stopped at the store and purchased a carton of Newports. She had no intention on leaving the house anytime soon. There was enough leftovers from the repass. Food, soda, water, and alcohol. "Get up!" what for? What do I have to do? Where do I have to go? Monuette rolled over in her bed once again.

What Monuette didn't know was that her friend and spiritual sister Sabrina had left a message yelling "GET UP!". Sabrina went on to say that if Monuette didn't answer the telephone or the door today she was going to bring a locksmith to pick the lock. Unbeknownst to

Monuette, Sabrina was now on her way to Monuette's apartment.

Sabrina and Monuette had been friends since childhood when they attended Sunday school at JCC. During High School they went their separate ways but remained cordial friends. When Monuette returned to JCC three years ago the ladies reconnected. Sabrina now married to assistant Pastor Andre Baez and the mother of twin boys Alvin and Arnold was truly a blessing for Monuette to have in her life. Never judging of Monuette, always patient, always understanding. She was just the friend that Monuette needed after being taken advantage of in the streets.

Yes the streets had done a number on Monuette, the church girl that thought she knew it all and was in control of everything. Not only had the streets broken her the men in her life had done so as well. Drug addicted and broken down she returned to her mother's apartment and to JCC. Monuette cried out to God for deliverance back then. Should she cry out to God for help now? Her heart was truly aching and at times she felt like she was sure to have a heart attack. She even welcomed a heart attack because she felt that she could not go on without her family. Monuette had even contemplated suicide. She wanted to be free of the loneliness, the pain and agony that she was feeling.

Boom, boom, boom!!!!!! Someone was knocking at the door. Who the heck would have the nerve to come banging on my door like this? Thought Monuette. Boom, boom, boom!!!!!!! Monuette sat up in her bed and listened for voices. Boom, boom, boom!!!!!!

"Monie!!!!!!! It's me, Sabrina. Open the door".

Monuette lit another cigarette and ignored the knocks. She wasn't aware that Sabrina had a locksmith with her. She figured Sabrina would get tired of knocking and leave. Boom, boom, boom!!!!!!

"Monie open the door!"

Monuette sat up in bed, pulled on her cigarette and cried. She cried because she missed her family. She cried because Sabrina had come to check on her. She cried because she didn't know how to carry on.

"Monie, I'm going to count to ten and if you don't answer the door I have a locksmith here to break the locks!" Sabrina yelled through the door.

Monuette knew that Sabrina was bold enough to bring a locksmith to her apartment so she decided to go to the door. She wasn't planning on letting Sabrina in though. She would let her know that she was okay but wanted to be alone. She got out of the bed and walked to the door with the tears streaming down her face.

"Sabrina, I'm okay. I just want to be alone." Her voice was dry and hoarse and she could barely hear herself speak.

"Monie, is that you? I can barely hear you. What did you say? Sabrina asked with concern.

Monuette tried to clear her throat.

"I said that I'm fine and that I will give you a call tomorrow."

"No! that's not part of the plan Monie! You open this door right now or I'll have the locksmith open it". Sabrina was adamant about getting into Monuette's apartment today.

Monuette opened the door and when they looked at each other they fell into one another's arms and broke down crying. Sabrina cried because her friend looked skeletal and she was afraid the Monuette might be back on drugs. What had she done in the past five days? Was she smoking crack? Sabrina squeezed Monuette tighter and realized that Monuette smelled really bad but she just held on and thanked God for another day with her friend. Another day to let her know of God's goodness, his grace and his mercy. Monuette held onto Sabrina right there in that doorway. In Sabrina's embrace Monuette felt hope, and she felt the love of Jesus Christ the Lord and savior of the world.

Sabrina thanked the locksmith and gave him $40 for his trouble then the ladies entered Monuette's apartment.

"Whew!" said Sabrina.

"I'm going to clean up while you get your stink butt in the shower". They both laughed.

"Okay" whispered Monuette. Her voice was barely audible.

After Monuette had showered the ladies sat and discussed everything that had happened in the past two months. Sabrina knew that it had been hard. In fact she had discussed this with her husband Andre. She didn't know what she would have done had the circumstances been hers.

"Monie, you have to push through! No matter how hard it gets, push through. Yes, bad things happen to good people and we know that the enemy comes to steal our soul and our destiny but you can't let him. Do you remember how broken you were when you returned to your Mom, to God and to JCC three years ago? You received deliverance then and deliverance is available to you now. God will send the comforter to you just as his word has promised. You just have to push through."

"Remember your mother's prayers they haven't went unanswered. Your Mom is in Heaven now but the prayers that she prayed when you went missing in those streets years ago were answered." Sabrina went on.

"Philippians 1:6 says being confident in this very thing that he who has begun a good work in you will perform it until the day of Christ Jesus. God is not finished with you Monie. You have a wonderful life ahead of you and three Angels in Heaven watching over you. So you cry because we know that even Jesus wept. So you cry but you push through and you remember that you have a family at JCC."

One last thing, the church wants to offer you a paid position as a grief counselor. The trustees have approved it already. So in addition to your job that you currently have as a drug counselor you are now JCC's first ever grief counselor and you get to make your own schedule. Push through Monie, there is sunshine past this storm. 'PUSH THROUGH'!"

Cathy

Cathy walked the aisles of the supermarket in a daze. She had just saw a young lady that she thought was her daughter Rayshelle. She approached the young lady.

"Sorry Miss my name is Alana".

Cathy hadn't seen her children Raymond and Rayshelle since 2005 when their Father's mother had taken them away from Cathy because of her drug abuse. As she walked the aisles of the supermarket the pain that she had let go of so long ago came over her like a flood. She left the cart and ran into the restroom. Once inside she went into the stall and cried. It had been awhile since Cathy let herself cry, but now as she sat in the stall the memories, the pain and the anger came back as she remembered how it all began.

Cathy was born in Macon Georgia in 1962 the only child of James and Bertha Mitchell. In the summer of 1982 the family moved to New York City so that James could take a job working with the Metropolitan Transportation Authority also known as the MTA. James' sister Rebecca lived at 104 West 138 street in Harlem. Rebecca was able to get an apartment for the family in her building. It was good for Rebecca to have her brother James around as she had three sons and her husband had died years ago in the Vietnam war. Not long after Cathy and her family had moved in and got settled Darnell, Rebecca's youngest son invited Cathy to attend a party with him and his friends.

On the night of the party Cathy came downstairs wearing a pair of green silk Gloria Vanderbilt pants with a matching blouse. On her feet she wore a pair of white snakeskin sandals and carried a matching handbag. She wore her hair in shirley temple curls. Darnell was impressed with her attire and proud of his cousin whom he considered to be a country bumpkin.

"Everyone this is my cousin Cathy, you know the one I was telling y'all about" said Darnell proudly as he ushered her over to the two Jeep Wranglers that were parked in front of their building.

"Cathy this is Tyrone, Gwen, Tonya and Raymond. You'll be riding with me and Tyrone."

Cathy offered her hand to each of them and said her pleasantries.

"This girl has manners" laughed Tyrone.

Cathy climbed into the back of Tyrone's jeep. Cathy was thrilled to be going to a club on 125th street. She had heard stories about the bars, clubs and the famous Apollo Theater.

When they pulled up to the Celebrity Club there was a line waiting to get in but Raymond walked straight to the front gave the bouncer some dap and they were ushered right in. Once inside they were escorted to the bar where Raymond ordered Champagne for everyone.

"Did I tell yall that my cousin will be attending City College in September?" Darnell said smiling.

Cathy blushed.

"What is your major?" asked Tonya.

"Business management" replied Cathy.

The Deejay was jamming and Cathy noticed that many of the people at the bar were sniffing cocaine out of dollar bills. It was evident that Raymond was well known, there was a continuous group of people coming to where they were seated in order to speak with Raymond. Gwen passed the dollar bill to Cathy.

"I've never done this before" said Cathy.

"I'll feed it to you, just sniff" said Gwen.

Just then Afrika Bambaataa's Planet Rock came on and the dance floor got packed.

"Who want's to dance?" asked Cathy.

"Wait up, let me take a hit and I'll dance with you" said Raymond.

Raymond snorted the coke, passed it to Tyrone, grabbed Cathy's hand and headed to the dance floor. After a while, Sister Sledge's song *He's the greatest dancer* came on and Tonya, Darnell, Gwen and Tyrone joined Raymond and Cathy on the dance floor. The DJ was rocking and they all danced to a few more songs before they headed back to the bar where they continued to drink champagne and sniff coke. When the party was over Raymond asked Cathy to ride with him. They all went out to eat at Midnight Express a 24 hour diner on Manhattan's upper Eastside. The night had been wonderful and Cathy thanked them all for showing her such a nice time. Afterwards Raymond dropped Cathy off and told her to be ready at noon because he was coming to get her to hang out with him.

"Okay, see you tomorrow" smiled Cathy.

Cathy and Raymond started spending a lot of time

together. Raymond rode around Harlem with Cathy in the front seat of his Jeep Wrangler. Cathy soon found out that Raymond was selling cocaine and that Darnell, Tyrone, Gwen and Tonya worked for him. Cathy's parents didn't like Raymond and Cathy's father warned her on several occasions about dealing with guys the like of him. It was already too late. Cathy was enjoying the gifts and the attention that she received from Raymond. They went out to party and would snort coke on occasion. Darnell warned Cathy of the dangers of sniffing too much coke because he did not want her to get addicted.

"It's okay to have a one on one from time to time Cuz but you can't do it every day because you'll turn into a cokehead just like these other girls and never, ever, ever freebase or you'll end up lost and turned out. I'm serious Cuz, I've seen it happen to the best of them" Darnell had told her.

It wasn't until 1994 that Cathy began to sniff cocaine on a regular basis when Raymond purchased a house in Connecticut for his parents and he and Cathy moved into his parents apartment in Lincoln Projects. At this time Cathy also befriended Stephanie and Joanie two young ladies that lived on her floor. Raymond was spending more of his time in Virginia where he had expanded his drug business so Cathy didn't mind having the girls over to her apartment when she had free time. They would sit and listen to music, do each others hair and nails and sniff coke. Cathy was happy to have friends of her own. She enjoyed hanging out with Gwen and Tonya but they were Raymond's friends and at the end of the day their alliance was to him.

In January 1995 Cathy found out that she was pregnant. Raymond was overjoyed he was now Thirty-eight years old he was thinking that he may be sterile because most of his friends had children already. Cathy's parents were ecstatic and spoiled Cathy even more than they had already done, however they wanted more for their child and they encouraged Cathy to ask Raymond about marrying her. Cathy stopped partying and doing drugs. Stephanie and Joanie would still come around looking for free coke and borrowing money and clothes that they never returned.

On September 21, 1995 at 2:14am, Cathy gave birth to a 7lb 9oz boy. Her Mom was with her in the delivery room because Raymond was out of town. When Cathy awoke the next morning Raymond was sitting in her room holding his son. Cathy smiled.

"When did you get here?"

"When your Mom called I got on the earliest flight I could get. I've been here for about a half hour" said Raymond.

"Come give me a kiss" Cathy said sleepily.

Raymond walked over to the bed and Cathy kissed him and the baby.

When Cathy got home from the hospital, Stephanie and Joanie started visiting her apartment again and Cathy would sniff cocaine with them. Raymond was spending more and more time in Virginia so he didn't know that Cathy had started sniffing coke again on a regular basis. On the weekends Cathy would take Little Raymond to her parents so that she could party and hang out in the after hours spots. Gwen and Tonya tried to warn Cathy about Stephanie and Joanie but after 13 years of living in Harlem Cathy was still as naive as she was the day they had first met her.

Cathy soon found out that she was again pregnant but this time she did not stop sniffing coke as she had done when she was pregnant with Little Raymond.

Raymond found out that Cathy was still sniffing coke and he threatened to take Little Raymond and the new baby when it was born if she didn't stop sniffing. Then he went to knock on the apartment doors of Stephanie and Joanie.

"Do me a favor, don't knock on my door anymore and stay away from my wife with your bum asses. I don't want to have to tell you again. Next time I'm not going to be so nice". Raymond turned and walked away.

"Those two won't be coming here anymore and if I find out that you are going over to their places I'm taking Lil Ray" yelled Raymond once he was back in the apartment.

"Baby you're always on the go. Lately you've been spending more time in Virginia then you do at home and I like having my own friends. Gwen and Tonya are your friends, I like having friends of my own. I just sniff coke because I'm bored and it's something to do to pass time" cried Cathy.

"Don't give me that mess Cathy. You're not sniffing because you're bored you're doing it because Stephanie and Joanie come over here everyday with their broke asses looking for a free high. I don't understand you, can't you see that they are just using you. Baby I love you and I only want the best for you." Raymond pulled Cathy to himself and wrapped his arms around her before he continued.

"Do you know how much I used to brag about you?" Raymond kissed Cathy on her lips and wiped away her tears.

"Do you remember how proud I was of you when you graduated from City College with your Bachelor's Degree? Cathy you are not like these other girls, don't get caught up in this hood shit. Why don't you go back to work since you say that you are bored. Ask your Mom to watch Lil Ray and I'll pay her for babysitting. Okay?"

"Okay" responded Cathy.

The following Monday morning Cathy went downtown to Access Per Diem services where she took a clerical and typing test. She did well and was told to go to John Street where she would be working as a junior underwriter for Scor reinsurance. She quit sniffing coke and was working really hard at being a good Mom and girlfriend. Raymond started spending more time at home with Cathy and Lil Raymond he also had Tonya pop up to check on them when he was out of town. Raymond was falling in love with Cathy all over again. One evening Raymond came home with a two carat princess cut engagement ring and proposed to Cathy. Cathy shrieked.

"YEEEES!!!!!" Cathy said jumping up and down.

"I have to call my mother" she ran to the phone.

"Ma, Raymond just proposed. You have to see my ring! It's huge! We have to start planning a wedding. Of course we're going to wait until after the baby is born. You know I have to look cute in my wedding gown. Okay tell Dad, you know how much he wanted me to get married. Okay good night, I'll see yall in the morning".

Raymond smiled, he was in love with Cathy all over again.

On September 5, 1996 at 7:05pm Cathy gave birth to a 6lb 7oz beautiful baby girl. This time Raymond was in the delivery room with her. In the waiting room was the whole crew along with Cathy's parents. Darnell, Gwen, Tonya and Tyrone all rushed to the maternity ward to be present for Raymond. Raymond had slipped the security guard a hundred dollar bill to let them all upstairs. Cathy decided to name her daughter Rayshell.

Rayshell was seven weeks old when Raymond got a call from Virginia and was told that he had to come right away because one of his spots had gotten raided. He tried to send Tyrone but he was unable to reach him.

"Baby-girl, I don't want to go but I have to. I couldn't really get into specifics over the phone you never know who's listening in. I've tried to reach Tyrone on his mobile phone, I called the bar, I called his girl and no one has seen him. I'm going to drive out tonight, see what's going on and try to get back on the road tomorrow night".

"I have a bad feeling about this. I wish you would stay home. Why can't you send Darnell?" whined Cathy.

"Baby-girl, not for nothing but you know Darnell is not built for times like this. He's a clown, he's my brother but for what needs to be done right now he's not who I can depend on".

Rayshelle started crying and Cathy walked over to the crib and picked her up. They had decided to put the crib in their bedroom so that Rayshell's crying wouldn't awake Lil Raymond in the middle of the night.

"Tell Daddy not to go" cooed Cathy.

"Now you're not playing fair Baby" laughed Raymond.

Raymond packed an overnight bag, kissed Cathy and the kids "I love you baby"

"I love you too. Hurry back I miss you already."

Cathy was awakened by the phone ringing.

"Hello"

"HE'S DEAD!, MY BABY BOY IS DEAD!!!, HE'S DEAD" cried Miss Betty, Raymond's mother.

"No Ma, he's not dead he just left here a few hours ago. He's on his way to Virginia to handle a few things. He'll be back tomorrow night" said Cathy.

"NOOOOOO!!!!! I just got a call from the State Troopers he was in a car accident on interstate 95. Cathy they said my baby is dead. We have to go and identify his body" Cried Betty.

Cathy hung up the phone on Miss Betty. She couldn't believe what she was hearing clearly Betty was mistaken. She called Raymond's mobile phone but couldn't get an answer. She tried beeping him and putting in 911 he would usually call right back if she put in 911. She called his mobile phone again but still didn't get an answer. Cathy was out of the bed and pacing the floor, her hands were shaking and her knees buckled she was now on the floor. Cathy called Miss

Betty back, Miss Betty answered on the first ring. Now it was Cathy's turn to scream.

"MA, HE DIDN'T ANSWER MY CALLS!!!!!!! THIS CAN'T BE HAPPENING. MA, TELL ME IT AIN'T SO!!!!!!!!"

Both women cried for awhile before they could discuss getting to Maryland where the accident had occurred. Raymond's father, Charles Thomas, was suffering with Alzheimer's disease and Betty didn't want to leave him alone but she also didn't want to take him on the drive to Maryland. It was decided that Cathy would take the children to her parent's apartment and she would ask Tonya or Gwen or both to accompany her to Maryland.

"Bring my baby back home to me Cathy. Money is not a problem so you do whatever it takes to bring my baby home so that I can give him a proper homegoing" cried Betty.

Raymond's parents came to stay with Cathy and the children as they prepared for the funeral and received guests. Tonya noticed that Cathy had stopped breastfeeding Rayshell and was making frequent trips to the bathroom so she approached Cathy.

"What's up?" asked Tonya.

"Nothing, what's up with you? Are you alright? Have you eaten today?" asked Cathy.

"I should be asking you those questions. I noticed that you're making a lot of trips to the bathroom. Are you sniffing again? I'm not judging you, I just don't want you to get out of control. Girl, I know that you are hurting right now I can't even imagine what you must be feeling. I commend you on how strong you are for Ray's parents and for your children. I just don't want you to get out of control".

"Yes, I have been taking a couple of one on ones but I got this. I'm good, thanks for caring about me and the kids. I just needed a little pick me up". Cathy hugged Tonya. "Thanks for everything. I love you".

"I love you too Cathy."

The funeral was held at Abyssinian Baptist Church on December 6, 1996. The church was packed with family, friends and business associates. Cathy kept looking around to see if Tyrone would show up. Raymond's father didn't know what was going on and that saddened Cathy all the more because Mr. Charles and Raymond had been very close. After the burial, family and friends gathered in the community room of Gwen's building. Cathy was surprised to see Stephanie and Joanie at the repast. She walked over to them.

"Thanks for coming. I know that Raymond spoke badly to yall in the past and it means a lot to me to see that you girls showed up for me. Please stop by the apartment when my in-laws leave so we can hang out. I miss yall."

Cathy hugged Stephanie and Joanie and kissed them both on the cheek.

"I know that he was just protecting you and the children. It's all good we're over it now. We'll come check you out when his parents leave. Do you need us to help serve food and drinks?" asked Stephanie.

"No we have that covered but thanks for asking. I'll be back to sit with y'all. Let me go chat with the family".

Several days after the funeral Betty and Charles were ready to return to their home in Connecticut. Betty wanted to take the children with her but Cathy explained that the children were too young in addition to the fact that Mr. Charles' mental health was declining. In fact, the night after Raymond's funeral Mr. Charles had left the house in the middle of the night searching for an ice cream parlor that he used to frequent. It was a coincidence that Stephanie just happened to be leaving an after-hours spot on West 136 street when she spotted Mr. Charles who was agitated and becoming very aggressive until Miss Betty came to get him.

"Ma, you already have your hands full with your husband. Why don't you give yourself some time to get home and settled into your usual routine. I promise the kids and I will come visit for a week or two. In fact. I'll drive up on New Year's Eve and we'll stay for a week. Okay?"

Miss Betty began to cry. "Yes, that will be fine. I'm going to miss you all so much. I feel like I'm saying goodbye to my boy all over again." Betty fell on Cathy's neck and cried.

After Betty and Charles left, Cathy fed and bathed the children and put them to bed. Cathy had a lot on her mind in addition to missing and yearning for Raymond. First of all, she had to send someone down to Virginia to collect Raymond's money. His business associate had come to New York for the funeral and given Cathy $56,000 and his assurance that there was more to come when the product was finished. Cathy had placed it in the safe that Raymond himself built into the floor of their apartment. Cathy had enough money in her checking and savings accounts. When she found out she was pregnant with Little Raymond she purchased term life insurance policies for herself and Raymond. She would soon receive a check for more than $250,000 from the insurance company. She didn't want the life of a drug dealer but she also didn't want anyone taking what rightfully belonged to her children. Cathy went to the bar and her living room and poured herself a glass of wine then she went to her stash and snorted a line of coke. The house was quiet and Cathy was lonely so she decided to call Tonya, Darnell and Gwen over for an impromptu meeting.

An hour later Darnell, Tonya and Gwen were at the door with a Christmas tree, lights, decorations and Egg Nog. Cathy cried when she saw it all. Raymond used to make a big deal about Christmas and every year he would purchase a live tree and decorations himself. It was sweet of Darnell to remember. Cathy closed the children's bedroom door and turned the radio to WBLS FM. The four of them talked about old times and told stories about Raymond and Tyrone. It was as if Tyrone had fallen off the face of the earth. No one had heard from him. His family filed a missing person's report, checked the hospitals, morgues and jails on a regular basis but still there was no word from Tyrone. It was as if they had lost both Raymond and Tyrone. At least they had closure in regards to Raymond but for Tyrone to have just disappeared without a word was a bit much for the crew to handle.

Cathy kept her promise and went to Connecticut to visit Raymond's parents. She was overwhelmed by all the memories of Raymond that the house held and she was sniffing and drinking daily to medicate the pain of his loss. Mr. Charles' behavior did not help the matter. Because of his dementia he continually talked about Raymond as if he were still alive and had frequent violent outbursts. Cathy was afraid for the children, herself, Betty and Betty's sister Laura who had recently moved in to help Betty with Charles. Charles however was more than a handful and Betty decided that she would soon place him in a nursing home that was near their house. Betty had lost her only child and her husband of 37 years. Charles was no longer the man that Betty had fallen in love with and married.

One morning Laura inquired about Cathy's behavior.

"Raymond confided that Cathy was abusing cocaine while she was pregnant with Rayshell and he threatened to take the children away. He was planning on moving out here with them but thank God she got herself together. She returned to work and was doing an awesome job at maintaining the household, according to Ray" said Betty.

"Well she is on more than just the wine that's in that glass Sis. We're going to keep our eyes on her" whispered Laura.

When Cathy returned home Stephanie and Joanie came to visit her one evening.

"Hey girls, what's good? Come in, come in. I was about to put the kids to bed. Go fix yourselves a drink. I'm already tipsy as you can see" Cathy giggled.

Cathy walked into the bedroom with the children, placed them in their beds and returned to her company.

"Yall want a hit?" asked Cathy.

"Umm, we want a hit but we want to smoke" said Stephanie.

"Well I have to turn on the humidifier if yall want to smoke a cooley"

"We don't want to smoke a cooley we want to freebase" said Joanie.

"Freebase? Yall freebasing now? When did y'all start doing that?

"We tried it about a month ago and we like it. Cathy it is the best high ever. You have to try it! I'll go get the pipe, cooking jar and baking soda from my apartment. It's not like crack with all that other shit in it. It's only baking soda, water and cocaine" said Joanie.

"What the fuck, go get it. I'll try it".

Now as Cathy sat in the bathroom stall and recalled how that one evening led to her downfall. Over a period of ten years Cathy's life changed drastically. Miss Betty and her sister Laura took the children away from her. Each time that Cathy tried to clean herself up the pain of what she had done to her children and to herself led her back to the drugs. On several occasions she attempted suicide and was once placed in Harlem Hospital's psychiatric ward. Cathy could not forgive herself and it was just easier for her to stay high than to face the reality of what her life had become. Her parents wanted nothing to do with her because after she spent all her money on drugs she stole from her parents and turned to a life of petty crimes to support her habit. Eventually Cathy ended up in prison. It was in Bedford Hills Correctional Facility during a prison ministry that she gave her life to God and forgave herself for what she had done to herself, her children and her parents.

"Good afternoon ladies, welcome to Open Door Ministries. My name is Evangelist Hall and it is my pleasure to be able to minister to you today. If you have your Bibles would you please turn with me to the Gospel of Mark chapter 10 verses 46 through 52. I will be reading from the Christian Standard Bible. 'They came to Jericho and as he was leaving Jericho with his disciples and a large crowd, Bartimaeus a blind beggar, was sitting by the road. When he heard that it was Jesus the Nazarene, he began to cry out "Son of David, Jesus have mercy on me!" Many people told him to keep quiet, but he was crying out all the more, "Have mercy on me Son of David!" Jesus stopped and said "Call him". So they called the blind man and said to him, "Have courage! Get up; he's calling for you." He threw off his coat, jumped up, and came to Jesus. Then Jesus answered him "What do you want me to do for you?" "Rabbi" the blind man told him, "I want to see!" "Go your way," Jesus told him. "Your faith has healed you." Immediately he could see and began to follow him on the road.'" Evangelist Hall finished reading the scripture and she continued.

"Let us pray. Father God I ask that you add a blessing to this word and also to the word in which I am about to minister to your children. I thank you Father for using me as a vessel to deliver the word to your daughters. It is in the mighty name of Jesus Christ that I pray. Amen."

"I was Blind Bartimaeus. Oh, I wasn't literally blind but I was spiritually blinded by life and the lifestyle in which I was living. My story is similar to many of you sitting here in this room right now. My husband and I were drug dealers during the 60's and 70's we sold heroin. In 1982 my husband was sent to federal prison for being part of a conspiracy. He died in prison ten years later from AIDS. After his death I began smoking crack and soon found myself sleeping in abandoned buildings. That's where my addiction took me. I wanted something different though! I prayed even in the midst of my addiction and I even attempted to go to church but I was too ashamed of my appearance and my odor. Then one day a group of women from a local community church were distributing food, bibles, clothing and feminine hygiene products. That night I went back to the abandoned building and instead of getting high I lit my candles and opened the bible to the book of Psalms. I read Psalm 70 verse 1 where it says Make haste o God to deliver me; make haste to help me O Lord. Then I prayed 'God please save me come quick'. You see I was told in the streets that I had a gift for gab but when it came down to conversing with God I was at a lost for words. I turned to Psalm 31 verse 9 where it says Have mercy on me Lord I am in trouble. I said that verse aloud over and over again and I cried and cried until I cried myself asleep. The next morning was Sunday I used the towelettes the women had given me to wash myself the best I could. I changed my clothes and I headed to the church. I stayed in that church all day long and like blind Bartimaeus I shouted out to God for deliverance. I wanted the scales lifted from my eyes I needed to see for I had been blinded for far too long. Satan had clouded my vision. I had not thought about the lives I was destroying when my husband and I were selling heroin. My husband and I looked forward to people overdosing on our product so that it could attract more business our way. We didn't care that it was someone's mother, father, sister, brother or child even. All we cared about was our money, cars, jewelry and clothing.

"Do you recall in the scripture it says that Bartimaeus jumped up and threw off his coat? He couldn't see the coat but it had provided him with a false sense of security. Something that he could hold on to though he couldn't see it. In the scripture it doesn't say that he picked up his coat and followed Jesus, no it says that he was able to see and followed Jesus on the road. Well, in a sense, I too had to throw off my coat and follow God. The high had been providing me with a false sense of security, it was my coat. So in that church that day I had the courage to jump up in front of that church and say 'Jesus, I want to see! I want to be saved!'" Tears were streaming down the face of Evangelist Hall and of half the women in the room including Cathy.

"I was saved that day in that church but you know what, I still needed saving from myself. I could not forgive myself whenever I thought I was getting it together by going to rehab and attending NA meetings along with attending church on a regular basis. I would still feel guilt for what I had done to my parents, siblings and friends. But most of all I couldn't forgive myself for what I had done to me." Evangelist Hall pointed at her heart.

One day that unforgiveness almost led me back to the drugs and to that abandoned building. I got down on my knees and I told God just how much I was hurting and asked for him to take away the pain. God lead me to 1 John 1:9 which says If we confess our sins, he is faithful and just and will forgive us our sins and purify us from all unrighteousness. So I decided right then and there that if his word says that he who is greater than I can forgive me for all that I had done then I could surely forgive myself."

When Cathy was released from prison she worked hard at getting her life together and forgiving herself. She made amends to her parents, tried to connect to Miss Betty and her children and got herself a job working at an insurance company. She also did some volunteer work with a prison ministry. She realized there in that stall that she was just having a moment. It wasn't the first time and she knew it would not be the last. What she was certain of though was that God was faithful and that he had not brought her this far to leave her. She had faith that one day she would see Little Raymond and Rayshelle again so for now she just said her favorite scripture aloud "Be merciful to me Lord, for I am in distress. My eyes grow weak with sorrow and my soul and body with grief." She came out of that bathroom stall, washed her face and hands and went on about her day with the confidence that God was with her.

About the Author

Monique Jones currently resides in Bushkill PA. Along with being an author she is also the owner and operator of Mobetter Mgmt & Catering. Monique Jones is a community advocate, tax professional and the owner/ operator of Mobetter Mgmt & Catering LLC. In addition to this book Ms. Jones also has a children's book entitled Prada & Paige.

Ms. Jones is currently filming a Christian Drama which she wrote and produced. HOW I MADE IT OUT THE HOOD.

www.ingramcontent.com/pod-product-compliance
Ingram Content Group UK Ltd.
Pitfield, Milton Keynes, MK11 3LW, UK
UKHW041918190726
13854UKWH00003B/1308

9 781684 713738